T0113535

Waiting Well:

A 21-day Writing Journey to Increase Patience

SHERYL WALKER

authorHOUSE®

AuthorHouse™
1663 Liberty Drive
Bloomington, IN 47403
www.authorhouse.com
Phone: 833-262-8899

Published by AuthorHouse 08/25/2020

ISBN: 978-1-7283-7065-1 (sc)
ISBN: 978-1-7283-7209-9 (e)

Library of Congress Control Number: 2020916466

To those that have been angels and allies during the waiting seasons,
Thank you.

INTRO

When we want something badly, we want it now: the job, the baby, the spouse, the breakthrough with our career, the breakthrough with our finances, or for God to make things right in a specific situation. During these moments, patience can be challenging to sustain. Waiting can feel frustrating and agonizing. Where is God? Patience without worry means "I trust you God." We forget that God is in control and makes moves in his divine timing, not in our man-made timeline. If he hasn't given us our request yet, it's because he knows it isn't what is best for us yet. He is still working to refine us before we receive his blessings. God has the final say in everything. It will all work for our good.

As I wrote this book, I reflected on my own life experiences, particularly my seasons of waiting. During those times, I felt I was making little to no progress. I would move forward a few steps and then backward even more steps. As I considered the anguish of the wait, I considered all I gained during those times. I came to see that there were blessings in the midst of what, at the time, seemed agonizing. In the end, these experiences increased my humility and dependence on God. Additionally, I refined what I was looking for, bonded with those on the waiting journey with me, relearned lessons from the past, and got extremely creative.

This text focuses on increasing patience through consistent daily reflection and writing. Daily writing often serves as an enlightenment ritual for me personally and refocuses me on what is important. Going through each day, one by one, forced me to look at all my waiting seasons as blessings. It forced me to seek out the joy in the journey. It shifted my perspective to consider what I gained through the pain of the wait.

This book was written during the 2020 COVID-19 pandemic, and when a series of senseless killings of black people in the United States sparked protests and looting. We are still waiting to return to "normal." There is an element of mourning during the wait. Many of us are wondering whether we will ever get back to normal. We must let go of this notion of "normal" and trust God as we await the "new normal." Rampant evil wasn't normal. Disconnection from our families, each other, and God wasn't normal. Nonchalantly killing black people wasn't normal. Was this a global awakening? What was God saying to us during the wait? Despite the season of uncertainty, we know God is here. He is always here, in the midst of the wait.

Structure:

In the subsequent pages, you will be presented with daily patience-building passages. These make up a series of 21 reflections on "waiting well," giving you meditations to carry out day by day. You will also be asked to write each day. Pour your heart out onto the pages that have been provided. Read, reflect, write, and wait well. I hope that you will benefit from this 21-day journey, and that, by the end, you will come to see the wait as an opportunity to strengthen your faith and glorify God.

Bottom line:

There will always be a waiting season, in some form. Get good at waiting. The joy is in fact in the journey. God builds us up with strength, wisdom, and faith as we surrender all and await his best for us.

"For I know the plans I have for you," declares the LORD, "**plans to prosper you** and not to harm you, plans to give you hope and a future."

- Jeremiah 29:11 (NIV)

Every good and perfect gift is from above, coming down from the Father of the heavenly lights, who does not change like shifting shadows.

- James 1:17 (NIV)

DAY 1

God Answers Prayers in His Divine Timing

There is often discomfort during the waiting season. Waiting can feel like an eternity. There are moments when you feel too stuck to even pray. The uncertainty takes over our every thought. The "what if's" overwhelm us. The worst-case scenario terrifies us. And sometimes the worst-case scenario in fact happens. Some of us also know that God uses the worst to produce the best, but even with knowing this, it's still difficult to get through. Perhaps things are slowed down by God because you aren't quite ready yet.

Transformation takes place during these seasons of waiting. Reflect on God's divine timing and all he accomplished in your life during the waiting seasons of the past. He is so precise that, even after devastation, he builds in seasons of healing, so you can recover from that challenge. If I am in a season of waiting on God, there must be a reason for the delay. He might be withholding information about what's next so you can focus on Him. With a little bit of a wait, the "thing" you are desiring might be even bigger, better, and grander than you anticipated. You might appreciate the blessing more because it wasn't so easy to come by. There might be things you still need to learn and solidify before the blessing appears. What is he perfecting in your character during this season? We must release control of knowing every detail of our lives and remember who controls it all. Your life is in God's hands. Focus on HIM, and not a man-made calendar.

Day 1 Prompt: Recall God's divine timing. Write three examples of God's perfect timing as it manifested in your life. Was it bigger, better, and grander than what you anticipated? What was God trying to reveal to you about his love during the waiting season? What aspect of your character did he develop during this season?

Do not be anxious about anything, but in every situation, by prayer and petition, with thanksgiving, **present your requests to God.**

- Philippians 4:6 (NIV)

DAY 2

Continue to Pray and Ask God for Signs

Prayer is a weapon for divine intervention. Prayer changes everything. Even when we don't have the motivation or strength to pray, God hears our cries and groans. Spend intimate time with God. Talk to him regularly. Ask God to build your patience as you wait.

Notice God's signs to stay the course or to make a move. It is vital to pay attention. You also have to have a relationship with God to know when and how he speaks to you. Remember, it's God's voice you must listen out for. What was the last thing he told you to do? Be open to the message in unexpected forms, such as a random coincidence, or something said to you by a complete stranger. God's message is often the still small voice that tells you…

Apply to this job…
Try for the baby today…
That person you just met, he's different, give him a chance…
She is your wife…
Hang in there, the engagement proposal is coming…
I am asking you to make this sacrifice before you get the blessing…
Don't keep knocking on that door. I'll open it at the right time…
Distance yourself from that relationship, and I will open up a window of blessings…
Release your dependency on that thing, break that bad habit, and I will do a new thing in your life…

You must pray, listen for his messages, and do the thing he told you to do to unlock the blessings. So, as we wait, thinking we are waiting on God, God is in fact waiting on us to pay attention. Wait on his cue to make the next move.

Get outside in nature. Go somewhere in solitude and talk to God. Ask him to show you explicitly what he wants you to do. He will direct your path.

A point to note: Your blessing might be right in front of you. You can become so preoccupied with acquiring the thing you have set your mind on, that you completely miss the blessing God actually sends you. Your husband might be the friend you are brushing off. The person you hired might be the help you begged God for on your journey. Don't overlook the answer to your prayer.

Day 2 Prompt: What have been some interesting coincidences and other messages from God as they relate to what you are waiting for? What is God trying to say to you through those messages?

_____

_____

_____

_____

_____

_____

_____

_____

_____

_____

_____

_____

_____

_____

_____

_____

_____

_____

Let us not become weary in doing good, for at the proper time **we will reap a harvest** if we do not give up.

- Galatians 6:9 (NIV)

All who are prudent act with knowledge, but fools expose their folly.

- Proverbs 13:16 (NIV)

DAY 3

Maximize your Current Placement

If you are still in this current state, then God has a reason for you to still be there. He might still have work for you to do. There might be some unfinished business. Maybe there is more for you to learn in preparation for the next assignment. Maybe you haven't done what he has asked you to do. There might be some relationships you have to reconcile and restore; therefore, you have to do the work to forgive or apologize. There might be some relationships you have to release. Perhaps God wants you to get organized and prepared. Get all the lessons you need to get from your current placement. Continue to learn, grow, and do good in the current place until the next assignment is ready to receive you and you are ready to receive it. Get things in order, so that when God says it is time, you can ease gracefully into your next season. Your new blessing will have its own set of challenges: prepare yourself for them.

Day 3 Prompt: Have you been maximizing your current season? If God were to move you to your next assignment right now, would you be prepared? Are you prepared for the blessing you have been praying for?

Then the Lord replied: **Write down the revelation** and make it plain on tablets so that a herald may run with it. For the revelation awaits an appointed time; it speaks of the end and will not prove false. Though it linger, wait for it; it will certainly come and will not delay.

- Habakkuk 2:2-3 (NIV)

DAY 4

Clarify Your Goals and Dreams, and Then Dream an Even Bigger Dream

What is it you are asking God to do? Write the vision and make it plain. Ask God for what you want. Praise him in advance for receiving it. Pray without ceasing.

Ask God to help you to clarify your goals. Don't limit God to just ordinary dreams. Dream a grand and audacious dream and allow God to blow your mind.

If you are feeling numb or apathetic, ask God to reignite your passion. If you feel unsure, ask God to reveal your purpose to you.

Consider writing goals for all the areas of your life: Family, Career, Spiritual Life, Health, Finances, Relationships, etc. Make this into a slideshow or vision board, or any visually appealing form. State specific criteria for the most ideal situation. Revisit this regularly. Start praying over these requests with specificity. Be as descriptive as possible.

Day 4 Prompt: Write down your goals. What is it you are asking God to do in your life? Be as specific as you can right now. What does your ideal job look like? Your ideal partner?

_____

_____

_____

_____

_____

_____

_____

_____

_____

_____

_____

_____

_____

_____

_____

_____

_____

_____

_____

_____

Always giving thanks to God the Father for everything, in the name of our Lord Jesus Christ.

- Ephesians 5:20 (NIV)

DAY 5

Count Your Blessings and Practice Gratitude

When the weight of the wait becomes overwhelming, pivot your attention from what you lack to something that needs your attention. Focus on all God has blessed you with. If he has blessed you before, he will bless you again. Continue to sow seeds of goodness and get prepared.

The law of attraction always holds true. You attract things to or away from you based on what you are focused on and how you feel. Proverbs 23:7 says," For as a man thinks in his heart, so is he." Let your feelings be your guide. If you focus on your lack, you are filled with sadness. If you are counting your blessings more than your problems, you will be in more of a peaceful place.

<u>Day 5 Prompt:</u> Gratitude T-chart

For one week, take notice of all your blessings (big and small) and all your frustrations. On the left side, track all the good things you take notice of. On the right, track how the enemy attempted to discourage you but it worked out. You will see that God is really for you and making moves on your behalf during this waiting season. There is a lot more that is in your favor than you might be seeing. What God is doing is far greater than the devil's tactics.

Gratitude T-Chart

BLESSINGS	ATTEMPTS AT DISCOURAGEMENT

Finally, brothers and sisters, whatever is true, whatever is noble, whatever is right, whatever is pure, whatever is lovely, whatever is admirable—**if anything is excellent or praiseworthy—think about such things.** Whatever you have learned or received or heard from me, or seen in me—put it into practice. And the God of peace will be with you.

- Philippians 4:8-9 (NIV)

DAY 6

Reprogram the Negative Autopilot and Speak Things into Existence

What do you allow your mind to say about you without your permission? If you don't exercise intentional authorship over your mental script, you might allow your mind to dwell on all the reasons to substantiate why you are unworthy of certain things: "I'm unworthy of x, y, z because…" or "See, it's my fault, I did not…". This is all from the enemy.

Negative thoughts might be exacerbated by questions people ask you or statements they make. Try not to be offended. Brush off the inquiry and focus on God's divine timing.

Controlling your mind is critical to waiting well. When your mind wanders to a dark and negative place, you have to pivot the thoughts to more positive statements. Replace negative thoughts with the thoughts you desire:

- I am a powerful person, and I have the job of my dreams.
- I am operating out of my gifting by (fill in the blank).
- I will have smart and supportive employees. The culture will support work/life balance. People will want to work there and stay there.

You have the power to create the life you want with your words and mental dialogue.

Day 6 Prompt: Rewrite the mental script here. How could a more positive autopilot sound? Speak your desires into existence.

As the body without the spirit is dead, so **faith without deeds is dead.**

- James 2:26 (NIV)

DAY 7

Do the Work. Keep Trying

If you are waiting on a new job, keep praying and interviewing. If you are waiting on the new home, keep searching and going to open houses. Nothing is in vain. Each interview prepares you for the next interview. Each open house clarifies what you are looking for in a home.

I recall working diligently looking for a new job for months with no success. Eventually, I decided it was time to take a break from my search and accept my current placement. As I was recovering from a series of rejections, the Holy Spirit said, "Keep interviewing," so I resumed the search. By the time I interviewed for the job I finally accepted, six months after my search originally began, the interview was a walk in the park. I was grateful for the many interviews that prepared me in advance for my God-ordained assignment.

Day 7 Prompt: How have you demonstrated diligence, persistence, and perseverance during the wait? In what ways have you taken action?

Look to the Lord and his strength; seek his face always.

- 1 Chronicles 16:11 (NIV)

DAY 8

Keep a Smile on Your Face and Remain Encouraged

If you have ever done something for someone and they were ungrateful or dissatisfied, you have a very small sense of how God must feel. Imagine he made us, his perfect design, in his perfect image. He had a plan for our lives from before we were even conceived. There has to be a rationale for this waiting period.

He develops us during the wait. We will look back on this time one day and be grateful for how he used the wait to develop our character. Wait patiently for the God that loves and cares for us unconditionally. He is the way maker. Smile, knowing that the blessing is surely around the corner. Use music and other means to lift your spirits and remain encouraged. Try your best to improve your mood. Feel good now.

You can be disappointed in God, but never stop trusting him. God has not forgotten your dreams, requests, prayers, or even your tears and agonizing pleas to him. He hears you and is working even in what appears to be his silence. Minimize impatience as best you can and remember who is in control. Dwell on God's goodness, what he has already done, and will continue to do. No time is ever wasted. He will bless you at the perfect time.

Day 8 Prompt: How do you remain encouraged during the wait (music, talking to a friend, etc.)? What is a memory that can remind you of God's goodness when it is difficult to keep smiling?

_____

_____

_____

_____

_____

_____

_____

_____

_____

_____

_____

_____

_____

_____

_____

_____

_____

_____

_____

But those who hope in the Lord will renew their strength.
They will soar on wings like eagles;
they will run and not grow weary,
they will walk and not be faint.

- Isaiah 40:31 (NIV)

DAY 9

Study Scripture and the Biblical Lessons of Patience

There are many in the Bible who had to wait on God. Let's look at a few examples.

Example 1: First, it took 120 years for the flood to happen after God instructed Noah to be prepared for it. Then, it took Noah over 100 years to build the ark. Then the rain poured down for 40 days. After the flood, they floated at sea for over 150 days. After the ark came to rest on solid ground, Noah waited an additional 40 days to test whether it was safe to emerge from the ark. He would send out a dove to see what it brought back, to establish if it was safe enough to exit the ark. Then, he spent about 60 more days to keep testing the dove and waiting on God's command. This is close to one whole year of waiting! It's worth remembering that one of the first things Noah did when he left the ark was to praise God.

Example 2: Job lost everything—his children and wealth in a single day, he had sores all over his body, and he endured. His friends falsely blamed him for his own suffering, and still he endured. Later, God provided double for his trouble, meaning his life was restored and he was provided with even more blessings.

Example 3: The Israelites endured over 400 years of slavery. Moses was charged with bringing them to the promised land, flowing with milk and honey. The journey took a long time, but God of course had a purpose behind that. He wanted the Israelites to learn to trust a new leader. Because of their complaining, dissatisfaction, and lack of trust, the journey was delayed. It took the Israelites 440 years to enter the promised land.

Believe God's track record. He will do what he says he will do in HIS right time.

Day 9 Prompt: What are some lessons we can glean from the biblical examples presented? Reflect on the themes of Noah's protection in the ark, Job's restoration, and the Israelite's lack of trust. Which story most connects to your current waiting season? Continue to study lessons in waiting through the stories of Abraham and Sarah, Jacob, and Ruth and Boaz. Also read and reflect on scriptures on the topic of patience.

Do to others as you would have them do to you.

- Luke 6:31 (NIV)

Therefore, as God's chosen people, holy and dearly loved, **clothe yourselves with compassion, kindness, humility, gentleness and patience.**

- Colossians 3:12 (NIV)

DAY 10

Extend Kindness During the Wait

Redirect your anger
Still be kind
Still be supportive

If someone is acquiring the thing you desire, such as the partner, new job, new business, or financial breakthrough, try to remain happy and supportive. Someone else's blessings does not prevent your blessings from coming to fruition. When it is your turn, you will want that same level of support and excitement. Always be generous with support and well wishes when it comes to someone else's success.

The energy you emit with jealousy is not in alignment with the positive energy you need to attract the blessings you desire. Wish people well on THEIR journey. If anything, throw the congratulatory dinner, baby shower, or house warming. Give them a tip to make them even more successful. Make the sacrifice. This is a test you might need to pass before your blessings come. Trust God: your blessings are also on the way.

Day 10 Prompt: Are you continuing to extend kindness during the wait? Are you still being loving and a blessing to others? What are ways you can continue to be supportive of those in your life who are obtaining the things you might desire?

"Do not store up for yourselves treasures on earth, where moths and vermin destroy, and where thieves break in and steal. But **store up for yourselves treasures in heaven,** where moths and vermin do not destroy, and where thieves do not break in and steal. For where your treasure is, there your heart will be also.

- Matthew 6:19-21 (NIV)

DAY 11

Don't Try to Make Your Own Plans Without God at the Center

Today we will continue our biblical exploration of those who had to wait, as we consider the notion of doing things on our own timeline when we do not get direction from God.

The case of Abraham and Sarah is a good example. God had promised Abraham and Sarah a child. Because they were already elderly, and Sarah had been barren until this point in their lives, they didn't completely trust God would honor that request. They waited and waited, but when things didn't happen within their timeline, they took matters into their own hands to fulfill what God had promised, which was to make Abraham a father of many nations. They decided Abraham should have a baby with Hagar, the maid servant. Things got complicated as soon as Hagar got pregnant. Sarah began to despise her. Then, after 25 years of waiting, Sarah was blessed with a baby named Isaac. At this point, relations had become so heated with Hagar, her and her son Ishmael had to leave Abraham's home. Impatience came at a cost.

Sometimes we feel pressured into taking a shortcut or making our own plans. No shortcuts. People will plant seeds in your mind that might make you want to expedite God's plan. For example, a couple that is dating might frequently be asked, "So when are you getting married?" Little do people know, they might have many issues to work through before marriage is a possibility. Rushing down the aisle without a clear understanding of your partner tends to not pan out well.

Day 11 Prompt: Are you beginning to seek a shortcut? Are external pressures enticing you to expedite this waiting season? What lessons can we glean from Sarah and Abraham's story?

_____

_____

_____

_____

_____

_____

_____

_____

_____

_____

_____

_____

_____

_____

_____

_____

_____

_____

_____

Jesus said to him, "Away from me, Satan! For it is written: **'Worship the Lord your God, and serve him only...'"**

- Matthew 4:10 (NIV)

DAY 12

Don't Allow the Desire for Something to Become an Idol

When we want something badly, we tend to have tunnel vision. That's all we focus on. You tend not to look up and around to see the blessings in front of you. Idolizing the acquisition of the thing, whatever it is, will consume your life. You will not take as much notice of the small blessings throughout the day, or how you are truly already blessed in a major way.

God strictly prohibits having idols over him. If the thing you desire is more of a focal point in your life than loving, serving, and praising God, then your priorities might be out of order.

Personally, I've found that I have obsessed over dwelling on the past during my waiting seasons. I would rehearse events in my mind. That too is a form of idolization and can lead to destructive habits. Try your best to focus on the present.

Day 12 Prompt: Have you made your desires an idol in your life? Do you think about acquiring this thing more than you think about God? What is this costing you? Peace of mind? Loving relationships?

Commit to the Lord whatever you do,
and he will establish your plans.

- Proverbs 16:3 (NIV)

DAY 13

Map Out Your Potential Path

The decision map I want to share with you is a combination of a decision tree, pros and cons list, and action plan.

1. Goals/Criteria
2. Decision tree
3. Pros and cons list
4. Action plan

First, look back at Day 4, when you clarified your goals. This includes the criteria for the ideal job, partner, house, etc. Second is the decision tree.

Decision tree:

This is a place to lay out ALL the different options most aligned to your criteria, with "yes" and "no" arrows. For example,

- If you are waiting for a baby, you might try to get pregnant, and if you've not been successful by a particular month, begin fertility treatments or the adoption process.
- If you are waiting for the ideal job, you might apply for a job in four fields. If the pay is over a set dollar amount within 20 miles from home, "yes." If not, "no."

- In matters of a job or relationship, your decision tree paths could be as simple as "stay" or "go."
- The decision tree will spell out certain contingencies with a "yes" or "no."

Pros and cons list:

Third, next to every yes, write out the pros and cons. For example,

- A pro of becoming a teacher is having summers off. A con is the starting pay.
- If you have been waiting for your engagement ring and it hasn't come, you might choose to leave. A pro is that you can begin looking for another partner. That is also the con. You might be better off having a conversation with your current partner instead of totally abandoning an otherwise good relationship.
- At this point in the process, you might begin to see smaller decisions you need to make, or the matters you need to clarify that connect to the even larger goal.
- This will lead you to have conversations with specific people or begin to refine your action plan.

Action plan:

Fourth, looking at things in their totality can now begin to set you up to take action. For example, now that you know which job might align most fully with your criteria, you might set out to

- Apply to 10 job opportunities. Make a list and check each off as you submit your information
- Reach out to a recruiter
- Reach out to all your connections in the field
- Ask certain people to serve as references for you

- Reach out to a specific doctor someone suggested, if you are trying for a baby or looking into a medical procedure
- If what you are waiting on is for pain to end, your action plan might include seeking therapy, reading books, journaling, or beginning to do some research into other potentially helpful measures you can take

Now get to work. Putting things in motion shifts your energy. As you go through the above steps, listen out for God. He is helping you as you chart this course.

Day 13 Prompt: Map out your potential path. Pray before beginning. Follow the steps outlined on the previous page.

Very early in the morning, while it was still dark, Jesus got up, left the house and went off to a **solitary place, where he prayed.**

- Mark 1:35 (NIV)

DAY 14

Breathe. Reduce Anxiety with Self-care

The push and pull of the waiting cycle often takes a toll on us mentally and spiritually. At times it feels like pure agony. How could God not help me out of this? God hears you, and nothing lasts forever. Breathe. Really focus on your breath. You are alive. You are surviving. Take things moment by moment.

I find often times our worst moments precede our best moments. Brighter days are ahead. Do whatever it takes to recharge your battery. Take a day off from work and engage in any of the following, or a combination of them:

- Spa Day and pampering: manicure, facial, massage
- Curl up in the bed with a good book
- Treat yourself to lunch at one of your favorite restaurants
- Take a fitness class
- Spend time or talk on the phone with a friend who puts your spirit at ease
- Make magical memories with loved ones
- Hang out with a baby and/or a puppy
- Hang out at a coffee shop doing whatever side project you are passionate about
- Retail therapy
- Spend time with your partner
- Tap into a spiritual outlet such as a church service

- Sleep
- Declutter
- Journal
- Pray on the hour
- Say thank you every half hour
- Take a break from people and situations that disturb your spirit
- Travel
- Spend time in nature

Day 14 Prompt: What have you done lately to care for your mental health? What do you plan on doing soon?

_____

_____

_____

_____

_____

_____

_____

_____

_____

_____

_____

_____

_____

_____

_____

_____

_____

_____

_____

_____

_____

Not only so, but we also glory in our sufferings, because we know that **suffering produces perseverance;** perseverance, character; and character, hope.

- Romans 5:3-4 (NIV)

DAY 15

Endure. Keep Pushing

Patience comes with long suffering. Hardships can last for much longer than it seems to make sense. Waiting strengthens us. No pain, no gain. You will be pushed. You will be tested. And you will make it.

As you wait, you might experience forms of rejection. This is just a distraction. Remember: rejection is God's protection. If you were rejected, that wasn't the best of what God could provide. If you feel you are going backwards, there is always the appearance of demotion before promotion. If you feel inadequate or unqualified, God qualifies the called. He will equip you with whatever you need. He will not bless you to then abandon you. If you feel frustrated, find healthy means to decompress.

God is the supplier of strength. God does some of his best work when you are at the end of your rope and wonder how you will make it. We discussed Job on Day 9. Job lost his family, wealth, and health. He endured, and all was eventually restored, and even more was added.

Consider a woman birthing a baby. She wouldn't stop midway, as the baby is beginning to move out of her body. It's the most painful part, but what's on the other side of labor? A beautiful miracle.

Again, take it moment by moment. This is exactly how it's supposed to feel. As was mentioned on Day 14, tap into opportunities to restore your strength and press forward. You can do this.

Day 15 Prompt: What are you most looking forward to on the other side of this waiting season? What are some sources of inspiration that you can tap into to help you to endure when the wait feels unbearable?

Be still before the Lord and **wait patiently for him;** do not fret when people succeed in their ways, when they carry out their wicked schemes. Refrain from anger and turn from wrath; do not fret—it leads only to evil. For those who are evil will be destroyed, but those who hope in the Lord will inherit the land.

- Psalm 37:7-9 (NIV)

Know therefore that **the Lord your God is God;** He is the faithful God, keeping His covenant of love to a thousand generations of those who love Him and keep His commandments.

- Deuteronomy 7:9 (NIV)

DAY 16

Guard Your Faith: Praise God and Thank Him in Advance

Has God ever left you? Hasn't he always been faithful? Meditate on your past victories. What would be different this time? Acknowledge his greatness and anticipate greater days ahead. Have hope and optimism. It's almost impossible to praise and worship God and be extremely impatient simultaneously.

Thank him in advance for the blessing you are about to receive. Don't block or miss your blessing with haste or ingratitude. What you are requesting is a process. We know how the story ends. Remain faithful. God always comes through in the most spectacular way. Wait on him.

He sometimes appears to be the "God of the last minute" or the "In the nick of time God." God likes to knock our socks off and truly make it clear he is the reason behind the miracle.

The waiting season is where you obtain your Faith PhD. You learn to truly trust him. And when "the thing" comes, it is an opportunity to glorify God for what only he could orchestrate.

Worship God gleefully as you wait, praying, praising, singing, and meditating on God with thanksgiving.

Day 16 Prompt: Speak as if you have received the thing you long for. Praise God NOW. Thank God for supplying it in advance of receiving it. On a scale of 1–10, where 10 is Abraham faith, where do you land? What is it that can move you along on the faith continuum?

_____

_____

_____

_____

_____

_____

_____

_____

_____

_____

_____

_____

_____

_____

_____

_____

_____

_____

_____

_____

_____

_____

Greater love has no one than this: to lay down one's life for one's friends.

- John 15:13 (NIV)

DAY 17

What Will Be Your Sacrifice?

We can't expect to always be on the receiving end of a blessing without putting in work and giving something up or becoming a little uncomfortable.

There are times in life it feels like God is negotiating or bargaining with us: If you do this, if you help out this person or if you outwardly forgive this person, I'll give you what you are asking me for. You must give up the fried foods, if you want a clean bill of health. You might have to sacrifice and pay a little bit more money if you want a more reliable employee. When I reflect on my life, my sacrifice has most often been giving of myself to patiently help others, or to forgive others even when still holding onto the pain of the offenses. Sacrifice also shows up for me as pushing through and sowing seeds of goodness despite challenging conditions.

When we consider the ultimate sacrifice—God giving his only begotten son to die for our sins—what are we going to do? The sacrifice you make during your extended wait might be tied to your next blessing. What are you willing to give, or to give up?

In the Bible, Abraham was promised a son. God gave him that son, and then asked him to sacrifice him. Abraham was willing to do it. He ended up not having to, but he was fully on board with obeying God's command. We can rest assured that we can give any and everything to God, because he is the same God that can instantly restore anything we have lost.

In another example, Moses was called to lead the Israelites out of Egypt. He sacrificed the comfortable life he would have had if he had not taken this role. This sacrifice resulted in millions of Hebrews being delivered out of Egypt. Mary gave up her reputation to give birth to Jesus. Blessings come with a price tag, but if you obey, the harvest will come.

Commit your whole life to living for God. Be humble and willing to sacrifice any and everything to be in obedience. Your sacrifice could be the catalyst to your next blessing.

Day 17 Prompt: Has God been prompting you to make a sacrifice? What are you willing to give, or to give up? A grudge? Pride? Your time to help someone who really needs you? Giving your knowledge and gifting in a certain area? What's your sacrifice?

_____

_____

_____

_____

_____

_____

_____

_____

_____

_____

_____

_____

_____

_____

_____

_____

_____

_____

_____

Submit to God and be at peace with him;
in this way prosperity will come to you.
Accept instruction from his mouth
and lay up his words in your heart.

- Job 22:21-22 (NIV)

DAY 18

Aim for Peace

Peace is always the goal. With all the noise around me, including my own anxiety and self-doubt, how can I rest assured knowing I am safely in God's hands?

Read the following passages and poems:

Patience (Part 1)

You must have patience,
You must wait it out,
As God builds your faith,
As God prepares you for the next battle.
God's timing is always right.
Would you rather things rushed and be ill prepared,
Or wait on God's cue?
When God says go,
That is when I go.
Sometimes you can appear at the back of the line,
Losing the race,
And with God's perfect timing, priming, grooming,
All things are possible.
Don't waste the season of preparation:
You have to be ready when God is ready for you to move.

Your harvest is waiting.
Stand firm in your faith that all storms are temporary,
All waiting is in preparation for your blessings.
Stay in the game of life as you await God's answer.

Patience (Part 2)

The waiting and the wanting cycle
Is a universal agony:
The job;
The love;
The baby;
The house;
The not feeling this way anymore…
Despite the knowing,
Despite God's track record.
The Faith-Trust-Patience Exam is here.
Not a perfect score,
But I know I've scored higher,
This time around.
I'm more at peace.
I know who runs this entire operation,
I've got inside connections,
Yet anxiety comes in waves.
The ebb and flow of panic and reassurance
As you recall God's past goodness,
You remind yourself of who you are,
And whose you are,
How his timing is perfect,
How "all things work together
For good to them that love God,
To them who are called
According to his purpose,"
And that "I have never seen

The godly abandoned or
Their children begging for bread,"
And you know that,
You really really really really know that,
Yet your humanity causes you to
Feel the weight of
Defeat,
Fear,
Discouragement,
And that is when we ask God to hold us in his arms
To give us that peace which surpasses all understanding.
My God,
My Rock,
My Salvation,
Let peace abide in me as I await victory

Patience (Part 3): The beach

There is a rocking motion to the beach.
We don't see the shoreline
Recede over time
Because we are lulled not to take notice of
The small changes.
The tides are turning in the waiting.
We may not see it,
But God is always in motion,
Even in the stillness,
The rocking,
The lull.

Have peace regarding the outcome. Don't be angry. Don't allow the enemy to keep you stirred up. Try your best to remain calm. Instead of focusing on the what, focus on the provider. God will always do what is in our best interest. You must believe that.

Day 18 Prompt: Are you at peace? Which poem or passage resonated with you the most? Why?

Be completely humble and gentle; be patient, bearing with one another in love.

- Ephesians 4:2 (NIV)

Love is patient, love is kind. It does not envy, it does not boast, it is not proud

- 1 Corinthians 13:4 (NIV)

DAY 19

Have Patience with People.
Pass the Patience Tests

If we could walk around and see everyone's hurt, scars, pain, abuse, and lack, we would probably have more compassion and patience toward them. Each one of us has a story. This is not to excuse bad behavior, but merely a point to remember as we engage with God's children. As God works on developing others, it can come across as strife and disobedience.

Humans are complicated and sometimes behave badly. When God wants to build patience in us, he sometimes surrounds us with challenging people or those that don't behave or support us in a manner that we wish they did. Remember: you cannot change people—only God can. God asks you simply to love them. Patience is an important part of loving people. You can only change yourself and how you operate within that situation.

If you are waiting for someone to change, you will have to reconsider that notion. Everyone is on their own journey, moving at their own pace. That is under God's plan and power, and no one else's. They may never change. All we can do is work on ourselves and pray for others. Don't put your own life on hold waiting for someone else to become what you would like for them to be. Again, you don't have that power.

Have patience for others, but with boundaries. For example, you can be gentle, loving, kind, and patient with others, but at the same time refuse to allow them to deplete you (mentally, emotionally, etc.), take advantage of your kindness, or wreak havoc in your life.

Also, remember that people have been patient with you at various points in your life. Maybe it was at your first job, or when you were going through an emotionally or spiritually transformative period in your life. A good measure to adopt is to do something to help the person who is testing your patience. Maybe God sent you along to teach them something important for their life journey. Patience with people usually translates to acceptance and forgiving people for their shortcomings and faults.

As you wait, you may face a few patience tests that include others around you. You will find yourself presented with people to whom you need to give some grace and mercy, or who you need to forgive or seek forgiveness from. Acknowledge the test. Forgive and apologize where you need to. Mend the relationships God is prompting you to mend. Your lack of forgiveness could be leaving an open wound when forgiveness could completely mend and provide healing for that other person. Passing the patience test could be the catalyst to your next blessing. Remember: everything we do is for the glory of God.

Day 19 Prompt: Have you been exercising patience with people? Are there individuals you need to be patient with, while still maintaining boundaries? What are ways you can gift others with patience?

_____

_____

_____

_____

_____

_____

_____

_____

_____

_____

_____

_____

_____

_____

_____

_____

_____

_____

_____

_____

_____

"Truly I tell you, unless you change and **become like little children**, you will never enter the kingdom of heaven."

- Matthew 18:3 (NIV)

DAY 20

Surrender

Truly remove your hands from the steering wheel. Give your whole life to God: every want and desire, every longing. Give the problems to him and then focus on Him. Talk to him through prayer and study his word. After you give it to him, be at peace. Know that there is an end date to this waiting season. This feeling won't last forever.

Let him do all the planning and rearranging. If you are trying and trying to no avail, the Holy Spirit might give you the message to cease pushing for the moment and enjoy where you are right now. Again, he never forgets a want. He fulfills all his promises.

The enemy wants you to waste time with worry. Worry means, "God I don't trust you." Don't fall for that trick. Waiting—and the agony of the wait—are parts of the journey. It isn't unique to you, and it is what each and every person needs to build their faith muscles. Anything that feels impossible is the opportunity for God to step in. Lift your hands in the air and say, "Lord, I surrender all."

Day 20 Prompt: Have you been working toward your desire with what appears to be minimal evidence of progress? Are you ready to give your want completely to God? What would surrendering look, sound, and feel like?

_____

_____

_____

_____

_____

_____

_____

_____

_____

_____

_____

_____

_____

_____

_____

_____

_____

_____

_____

_____

But **grow in the grace and knowledge of our Lord** and Savior Jesus Christ. To him be glory both now and forever! Amen.

- 2 Peter 3:18 (NIV)

DAY 21

The Metamorphosis

Waiting changes us. Like the butterfly, we go through different stages. The butterfly begins as an egg, then a caterpillar, then forms the cocoon, and eventually becomes a butterfly. Patience is required for anything worthy to manifest.

Similarly, all the pain, all the uncertainty becomes something beautiful one day— a dream come true, a testimony, or simply the ability to relate to someone enduring the same agony you once experienced. You might then serve as a source of comfort. Maybe it shows you that you are not in control and increases your dependency on God. We always strengthen our faith during the wait, and for that alone we have to be immensely grateful. The pain always has a purpose.

Be patient with yourself. One day you will see how waiting is the ultimate love message from God: "I love you this much I want to give you the best, and when you receive it, I want you to be at your best." He refines us during the wait. We get stronger, wiser, and more faithful. Thank you, God, for loving me this much, that you want me at my best. Thank you, God, for transforming me during the wait.

Day 21 Prompt: What changes have you seen in yourself during this waiting season? In what ways are you stronger, wiser, and more faithful? How have you evolved?

CONCLUSION

If God makes us wait, then it's worth the wait. Great things are always worth the wait. I recall hearing a sermon from Joel Osteen where he referenced the notion that a blessing that is given too soon is not God's best. He used the analogy of the pregnancy of an elephant versus a dog. An elephant is pregnant for two years. Since an elephant is so big, it takes a longer time for a baby to grow and develop in the womb. Conversely, a dog is pregnant for around two months and gives birth to multiple puppies, up to seventeen. To birth one elephant takes 730 days, and to birth seventeen puppies is 63 days. That is almost twelve times as long as a dog's pregnancy. The elephant is carrying an extraordinary blessing, something so big and special.

What you are about to birth takes time to grow and develop. Do the work and keep trying. Each new blessing will have its own set of burdens. Getting to point B might be the beginning of another season of challenges. It is best to be fully equipped for what God has in store for you.

Remember: the joy is in the journey from point A to point B. If your wait is filled with misery, you are not enjoying the journey. You have to remember life is not easy, but it is beautiful. You have to look at life differently. Smile and be grateful for what you have and for what you are learning about God during this season. Speak words of encouragement during this season. Continue to be kind. Map things out and do the best you can to get all you can in your current season to prepare you for your next season. Don't be so focused on your next season that you completely miss the current season.

Nothing lasts forever, good and bad. Recall the countless biblical examples. You will move to a new phase soon enough. Focus on God. Pray. Get focused and clear on what you are asking God to do. Be courageous and willing to wait patiently for God's divine timing. Breathe. God hears you. Endure. Make sacrifices. Have patience with others. Remain faithful, peaceful, and praise him in advance. Surrender all. You will be forever changed, when you have authentically experienced the mighty works of God and God alone. I wish you the peace that surpasses all understanding, as you wait on God.

ABOUT THE AUTHOR

Sheryl Walker is an educator and has facilitated 100+ one-on-one adult coaching conversations. Her writing is inspired by her own life journey and those she has coached professionally. Her books are centered around personal growth through the acquisition of new learning, self-reflection, and daily writing. Daily writing has often served as an enlightenment ritual for her personally as a way to endure life's most challenging moments. She is also the author of the books *Forgive Anyway: A 30-day Writing Journey to Total Forgiveness,* and *Love Poems to God.* She enjoys writing in her leisure.